TO

FROM

DATE

FOR MY GRANDCHILD

FOR MY GRANDCHILD

A GRANDPARENT'S GIFT OF MEMORY

An Imprint of Sterling Publishing Co., Inc.
1166 Avenue of the Americas
New York, NY 10036

ISBN 978-1-4549-2709-9

Distributed in Canada by Sterling Publishing Co., Inc.
c/o Canadian Manda Group, 664 Annette Street
Toronto, Ontario, M6S 2C8, Canada
Distributed in the United Kingdom by GMC Distribution Services
Castle Place, 166 High Street, Lewes, East Sussex, BN7 1XU, England
Distributed in Australia by NewSouth Books
45 Beach Street, Coogee, NSW 2034, Australia

For information about custom editions, special sales, and premium and corporate purchases, please contact Sterling Special Sales at 800-805-5489 or specialsales@sterlingpublishing.com.

Manufactured in China

2 4 6 8 10 9 7 5 3

sterlingpublishing.com
larkcrafts.com

All illustrations by Kaliaha Volha/Shutterstock.com except:
©Studio Barcelona/iStock 79; ©Tharnthip/iStock 24, 54

TABLE OF CONTENTS

A NOTE TO THE GRANDPARENT

When you're a grandparent, you play many roles in your grandchild's life—partner-in-crime, mentor, favorite babysitter, hero. But perhaps one of the most important roles is that of a storyteller. In fact, the story of your life is one of the most precious gifts that you can give. Whether it's a favorite childhood memory or a gripping account of your wildest adventure, the experiences and insights that you share strengthen the special bond that you have with your grandchild.

This is where *For My Grandchild* comes in. With fun questions voiced from the perspective of a curious grandchild to guide you, these pages offer a place to record your family's favorite traditions and chronicle the fads and fashions that were popular when you were growing up. You'll have opportunities to describe the milestones in your life and pass down practical advice that your grandchild will turn to again and again. There's also plenty of space in each section and extra pages at the back of the book for photos and mementos—share black-and-white and color snapshots, create a lively collage, or simply use the space to write anything you want. Many of the questions come with prompts to help you get started, but you are always welcome to skip the questions that don't apply to you or modify the prompts to your liking. Make this book truly your own.

By the time you reach the last page, you'll have created a heartfelt keepsake that brings your story to life. Your grandchild will have lots of fun learning about one of the favorite people in his or her life and will cherish the memories, experiences, and insights that you've collected for years to come.

A GIFT FROM YOUR GRANDPARENT

Why did you create this book for me?

_____

_____

_____

_____

_____

PUT A PHOTO OF YOU AND
YOUR GRANDCHILD HERE.

TELL ME ABOUT YOURSELF

Your name

(first, middle, last)

How did your parents decide on your name? Are you named after anyone?

Do you have any nicknames? How did you get them?

I call you _____. Where does that name come from?

Who are you, besides my grandparent?

Businessperson, traveler, photographer, hiker, musician?

YOUR CURRENT FAVORITES

BOOKS (OR OTHER THINGS TO READ)

MUSIC

VACATION SPOTS

GAMES AND HOBBIES

SPORTS TO PLAY OR WATCH

MOVIES

TV SHOWS

FOODS

ANIMALS

COLORS

DAYS OF THE WEEK

THINGS TO COLLECT

POLITICAL, RELIGIOUS, OR SOCIAL CAUSES

THE BEST PART ABOUT YOUR CURRENT AGE

OUR FAMILY

ME (YOUR GRANDCHILD)

....
NAME

....
BIRTHDATE

....
PLACE OF BIRTH

MY PARENTS

....
NAME

....
BIRTHDATE

....
PLACE OF BIRTH

....
NAME

....
BIRTHDATE

....
PLACE OF BIRTH

MY GRANDPARENTS (YOU)

....
NAME

....
BIRTHDATE

....
PLACE OF BIRTH

....
NAME

....
BIRTHDATE

....
PLACE OF BIRTH

MY GREAT-GRANDPARENTS

....
NAME

....
NAME

....
BIRTHDATE

....
BIRTHDATE

....
PLACE OF BIRTH

....
PLACE OF BIRTH

MY GREAT-GREAT-GRANDPARENTS

....
NAME

....
NAME

....
BIRTHDATE

....
BIRTHDATE

....
PLACE OF BIRTH

....
PLACE OF BIRTH

....
NAME

....
NAME

....
BIRTHDATE

....
BIRTHDATE

....
PLACE OF BIRTH

....
PLACE OF BIRTH

WHAT IS MY HERITAGE?

Where are my ancestors from?

_____

_____

_____

_____

When did they come to this country, and why?

_____

_____

_____

_____

Where did they settle, and what did they do there?

_____

_____

_____

_____

PUT PHOTOS AND MEMENTOS
OF OUR ANCESTORS ON THIS PAGE.

Tell me about your grandparents (my great-great-grandparents).

Where did they grow up? What did they do for a living, and how many kids did they have?
What do you remember most about them?

ON YOUR MOTHER'S SIDE:

....

....

....

....

....

....

ON YOUR FATHER'S SIDE:

....

....

....

....

....

....

PUT PHOTOS OF YOUR
GRANDPARENTS ON THIS PAGE,
AND ADD CAPTIONS IF YOU LIKE.

Tell me about your parents (my great-grandparents).

Where did they grow up? How did they earn their living?

_____

_____

_____

_____

_____

_____

_____

What's something you'd like me to know about your parents?

_____

_____

_____

_____

_____

_____

What were the most important things that you learned from them?

_____

_____

_____

_____

_____

_____

_____

_____

PUT PHOTOS OF YOUR
PARENTS ON THIS PAGE, AND ADD
CAPTIONS IF YOU LIKE.

What about your brothers and sisters (my great-aunts and great-uncles)?

Did you get along when you were growing up? What did you do together for fun? What's the most trouble you ever got into together (and what happened when your parents found out)? If you were an only child, what was that like? Tell me about your cousins or friends.

....

....

....

....

....

....

....

....

....

....

MY GREAT-AUNTS AND GREAT-UNCLES

Name: Name:

Birthdate: Birthdate:

Place of birth: Place of birth:

Name: Name:

Birthdate: Birthdate:

Place of birth: Place of birth:

PUT PHOTOS OF YOUR
SIBLINGS ON THIS PAGE, AND ADD
CAPTIONS IF YOU LIKE.

PUT PHOTOS OF OUR
FAMILY ON THIS PAGE, AND ADD
CAPTIONS IF YOU LIKE.

Tell me more about our family.

Which of our relatives does everyone consider most interesting?
What are your favorite family moments?

_____

_____

_____

_____

_____

_____

_____

Who are the best family storytellers, and what do they talk about?

_____

_____

Who am I most like, and why?

_____

_____

Is there anyone famous (or infamous) in our family?

_____

_____

WHEN YOU WERE LITTLE

Where did you live?

Was it a house, an apartment, or a farm? What was the area like? Did you move around a lot?

....

....

....

....

....

....

What was your family life like?

Were your parents strict? What were some household rules?
What did your family do for vacations or outings? Did you have family pets?

....

....

....

....

....

PUT PHOTOS OF YOURSELF
WHEN YOU WERE GROWING UP ON THIS PAGE,
AND ADD CAPTIONS IF YOU LIKE.

Tell me about elementary school.

What subjects and activities did you like most in school? What did you like the least?
Were you shy or outgoing? Did you have a favorite teacher?

What about activities outside of school?

Did you take any lessons, such as piano or dance? Did you play sports?
What were your favorite toys, books, songs, or TV shows?

PUT PHOTOS AND MEMENTOS FROM
ELEMENTARY SCHOOL ON THIS PAGE.

Who were your childhood friends?

What games did you play with them? Where was your favorite place to spend time together?

_____

_____

_____

_____

_____

_____

Who were your heroes?

What did you admire most about them? Did you have heroes who were characters from books, movies, or TV shows?

_____

_____

_____

_____

What did you daydream about being or doing when you grew up?

What were you looking forward to the most? Did these daydreams influence your future career goals?

_____

_____

_____

_____

PUT PHOTOS AND MEMENTOS
OF YOUR CHILDHOOD ON THIS PAGE.

WHEN YOU WERE A TEENAGER AND YOUNG ADULT

What were you like in high school?

What were your favorite subjects? Did you participate in any activities?
Who was your favorite teacher, and what made him or her so special? Were you a good student?

_____

_____

_____

_____

_____

How did you spend your summer vacations?

Did you go to summer camp? Did you work or volunteer?

_____

_____

_____

_____

_____

PUT PHOTOS AND MEMENTOS
OF HIGH SCHOOL ON THIS PAGE.

Tell me about your social life.

What were the biggest social events? What were some of the most fun (or wildest) things you and your friends did? Did you have an allowance or a curfew?

_____

_____

_____

_____

_____

_____

_____

_____

What about dating?

Where did you go on dates? Do you remember your first date?

_____

_____

_____

_____

_____

_____

_____

PUT PHOTOS OF YOURSELF
AS A TEENAGER ON THIS PAGE, AND ADD
CAPTIONS IF YOU LIKE.

What were the popular hangouts?

How much time did you spend there? Can you still visit them today?

Did you learn how to drive?

Who taught you, and how did that go? If you didn't learn, did you take public transportation,
bike, or get rides from your parents or friends instead?

PUT PHOTOS AND MEMENTOS
ON THIS PAGE.

What was cool to wear and do?

Clothes? Haircuts? Popular catchphrases? Did you think you were cool back then?

_____

_____

_____

_____

_____

What kind of music did you listen to?

Who were your favorite singers or bands? How about favorite songs? Did you go to a lot of concerts?

_____

_____

_____

_____

What was going on in the world?

Were you active in any social or political causes? Were there famous people—political leaders, activists, artists—who had a big influence on you?

_____

_____

_____

_____

PUT PHOTOS AND MEMENTOS
ON THIS PAGE.

Did you pursue a career right after high school or college?

What were some of your earliest jobs?

_____

_____

_____

_____

_____

_____

_____

_____

If you did attend college, tell me more about it.

Where did you go? What was your major? What activities were you involved in?
What were you like—studious, the life of the party, or something else?

_____

_____

_____

_____

_____

_____

_____

_____

PUT PHOTOS OF YOURSELF
AS A YOUNG ADULT ON THIS PAGE,
AND ADD CAPTIONS IF YOU LIKE.

WHEN YOU WERE ON THE JOB

How did you end up in your line of work?

*Did you know from an early age that you would end up in your chosen profession?
Was it difficult to get there?*

....

....

....

....

What was most rewarding about the work you did? What was most challenging?

Did you have a project that you were proud of? Were there tasks that you disliked doing?

....

....

....

....

Did you make any major career decisions?

*Was there a time you decided to switch from one field to another?
Did you leave a job so that you could take care of your family?*

....

....

....

....

Did you serve in the military?

What was your rank, and where did you serve? What type of work did you perform?
What was most memorable about your experiences?

_____

_____

_____

_____

_____

_____

_____

When did you retire? Or are you still working?

What is your favorite part about retirement? What is your favorite part about working?

_____

_____

_____

_____

_____

_____

WHEN YOU MARRIED

How did you meet my grandmother or grandfather?

Where did you go on your first date? What first attracted you to each other?

_____

_____

_____

_____

_____

_____

_____

How did you propose? Or how were you proposed to?

What did your parents say when you told them you were getting married? How long were you engaged?

_____

_____

_____

_____

_____

YOUR WEDDING

DATE AND TIME

PLACE

MEMBERS OF THE WEDDING PARTY

BEST (OR FUNNIEST, OR MOST NERVE-RACKING) MEMORY

SONGS PLAYED

HONEYMOON

PUT A WEDDING PHOTO
ON THIS PAGE.

BECOMING A PARENT

Tell me about when my parent was born.

When and where did it happen? What do you remember about that day?
How did you choose my parent's name?

....

....

....

....

....

....

....

....

PUT A PHOTO OF
YOURSELF AS A
YOUNG PARENT ON
THIS PAGE.

What was my parent like as a small child?

What were some things my parent did that made you happy? How about something that drove you crazy? What did you think my parent might grow up to be?

....

....

....

....

What are some of the things you like best about being a parent?

Is there anything that you miss about parenting a young child? What are some things you like best now that my parent is an adult?

....

....

....

....

What are some of the toughest things about being a parent?

When my parent was young, what were the day-to-day and long-term challenges? How did you handle them?

....

....

....

....

PUT PHOTOS OF YOU AND
YOUR CHILD ON THIS PAGE,
AND ADD CAPTIONS IF YOU LIKE.

In what ways do I remind you of my parent?

_____
_____
_____
_____
_____

In what ways am I different?

_____
_____
_____
_____
_____

What makes you proud of my parent today?

_____
_____
_____
_____
_____

BECOMING A GRANDPARENT

How did my parents tell you I was on the way, and what was your reaction?

_____

_____

_____

_____

_____

_____

When did you first meet me?

Do you remember how you felt when you held me for the first time? Did you brag about me afterward? Did you think I resembled anyone in the family?

_____

_____

_____

_____

_____

PUT PHOTOS OF YOU AND YOUR
GRANDBABY ON THIS PAGE.

What do you like best about being a grandparent?

....

....

....

....

....

....

What has surprised you?

How is it different from being a parent?

....

....

....

....

....

....

How has it changed you?

....

....

....

....

PUT PHOTOS OF YOU AND
YOUR GRANDCHILD ON THIS PAGE,
AND ADD CAPTIONS IF YOU LIKE.

A TYPICAL DAY

 THEN

When you were ____ years old, what was your daily routine on a weekday?

_____

_____

_____

_____

What was your daily routine on a weekend?

_____

_____

_____

_____

What were your favorite parts of the day?

_____

_____

_____

_____

NOW

What is your weekday routine like now?

_____

_____

_____

_____

What is your weekend routine like now?

_____

_____

_____

_____

What are your favorite parts of the day?

_____

_____

_____

_____

WHERE YOU'VE LIVED

Where did you first live as an adult?

What was the area like? Was it different from the place you grew up? Did you live with anyone else?

....

....

....

....

How did you decide where you wanted to live?

Did you want to stay near your hometown or move far away?

....

....

....

....

Where was your favorite place to live?

What did you like about it?

....

....

....

....

PUT PHOTOS OF YOU IN THE PLACES
YOU'VE LIVED ON THIS PAGE,
AND ADD CAPTIONS IF YOU LIKE.

WHERE YOU'VE TRAVELED

What are some favorite places that you've traveled to?

*Who did you travel with? What did you see and do while you were there?
What did you like about these places?*

_____

_____

_____

_____

What do you remember most about your trips?

What are the most beautiful sights that you've seen? Have you had any scary moments?

_____

_____

_____

_____

What is a place you'd like to return to?

What is special about it?

_____

_____

_____

_____

Is there a new place you'd like to visit in the future?

What would you see or do?

....

....

....

....

....

PUT PHOTOS OR MEMENTOS OF YOUR
TRAVELS ON THIS PAGE.

A MAP OF YOUR WORLD

Tell me some of the most memorable places you've lived and traveled,
what years you were there, and what you were doing.

Were you going to school? Maybe starting your first job? Were you traveling outside the country for the first time?

1

PLACE

DATES YOU WERE THERE

WHAT YOU WERE DOING

2

PLACE

DATES YOU WERE THERE

WHAT YOU WERE DOING

3

PLACE

DATES YOU WERE THERE

WHAT YOU WERE DOING

4

PLACE

DATES YOU WERE THERE

WHAT YOU WERE DOING

5

PLACE

DATES YOU WERE THERE

WHAT YOU WERE DOING

6

PLACE

DATES YOU WERE THERE

WHAT YOU WERE DOING

7

PLACE

DATES YOU WERE THERE

WHAT YOU WERE DOING

8

PLACE

DATES YOU WERE THERE

WHAT YOU WERE DOING

HERE AND NOW

PLACE

DATE YOU MOVED HERE

WHAT YOU'RE DOING

USING THE
CORRESPONDING
NUMBERS FOR
EACH LOCATION
ON THE PREVIOUS
PAGE, PLOT EACH
PLACE ON THE
MAPS.

TRADITIONS

Of all the holidays our family celebrates, which are your favorites?

How do we celebrate these holidays? Where do our traditions come from?

_____

_____

_____

_____

_____

_____

What are some of our favorite family customs?

What is unique about these customs? What do you like most about them?

_____

_____

_____

_____

_____

_____

PUT PHOTOS AND MEMENTOS OF
OUR TRADITIONS ON THIS PAGE.

What are the traditions you would most like to pass on to me?

Why are these traditions important to you?

....

....

....

....

....

....

Have any of our traditions changed since you were younger?

Which parts are different?

....

....

....

....

....

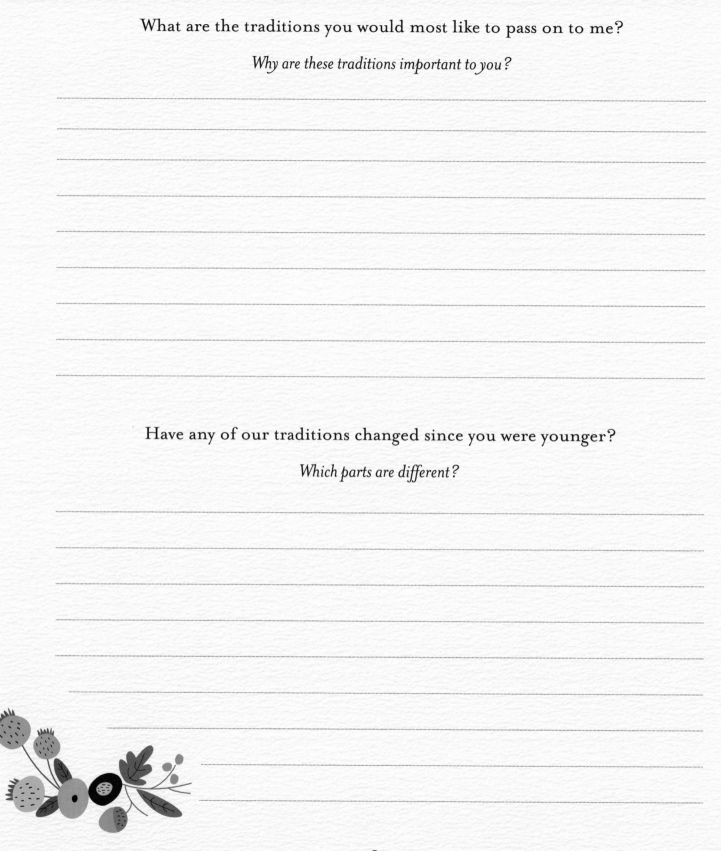

What family dishes do we always serve?

Are there any we always make for special occasions?

....
....
....
....
....

What is your favorite home-cooked meal?

Are there any foods that always remind you of home or your childhood?

....
....
....
....
....

Where does our family go when we have special celebrations?

Is there a restaurant that we always eat at? Are there family members who like to host special events?

....
....
....
....

63

FAVORITE FAMILY RECIPES

Recipe name: _____

Ingredients:

Directions:

Recipe name: _____

Ingredients:

Directions:

Recipe name: _____

Ingredients: Directions:

_____   _____

_____   _____

_____   _____

_____   _____

_____   _____

_____   _____

_____   _____

Recipe name: _____

Ingredients: Directions:

_____   _____

_____   _____

_____   _____

_____   _____

_____   _____

_____   _____

YOUR FIRST . . .

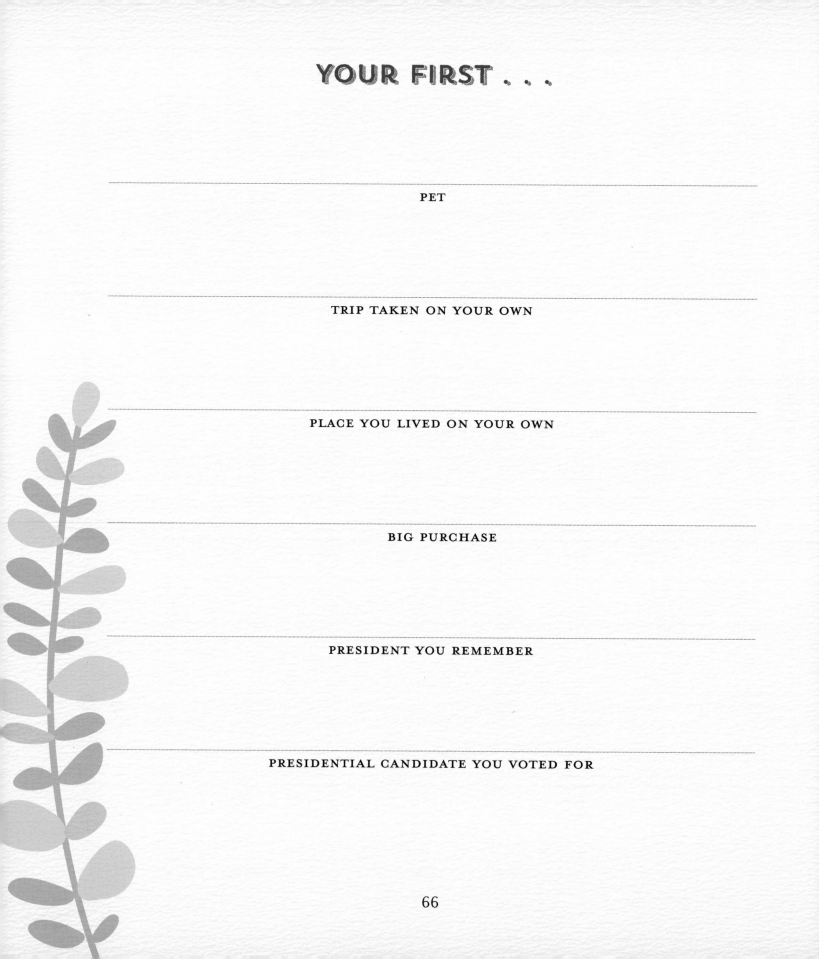

PET

TRIP TAKEN ON YOUR OWN

PLACE YOU LIVED ON YOUR OWN

BIG PURCHASE

PRESIDENT YOU REMEMBER

PRESIDENTIAL CANDIDATE YOU VOTED FOR

PUT PHOTOS AND MEMENTOS
ON THIS PAGE.

FAVORITE . . .

CHILDHOOD MEMORY

_____

_____

_____

_____

THING ABOUT YOURSELF

_____

_____

_____

THING YOU'VE CREATED, MADE, OR WRITTEN

_____

_____

_____

_____

COMPLIMENTS YOU'VE RECEIVED

_____

_____

_____

_____

QUOTE

PIECE OF ADVICE

TIMES SPENT WITH YOUR CHILDREN

TIMES SPENT WITH ME

MOST IMPORTANT . . .

_____

WORLD LEADERS IN YOUR LIFETIME

_____

SOCIAL MOVEMENTS IN YOUR LIFETIME

_____

POP CULTURE ICONS IN YOUR LIFETIME

_____

SCIENTIFIC DISCOVERIES IN YOUR LIFETIME

_____

INVENTIONS IN YOUR LIFETIME

_____

WORKS OF ART, FILM, OR LITERATURE IN YOUR LIFETIME

_____

WORLD EVENT IN YOUR LIFETIME—ONE SO IMPORTANT THAT
YOU REMEMBER EXACTLY WHERE YOU WERE WHEN YOU LEARNED OF IT

PUT PHOTOS AND MEMENTOS
ON THIS PAGE.

BIGGEST . . .

ADVENTURES

....

....

ADVENTURES YOU'D STILL LIKE TO HAVE

....

....

RISKS TAKEN

....

....

LESSONS LEARNED

....

....

SURPRISES ENCOUNTERED

....

....

ACCOMPLISHMENT

....

....

PUT PHOTOS AND MEMENTOS
ON THIS PAGE.

PERSON WHO . . .

YOU LOOKED UP TO MOST AS A CHILD

PLACE A PHOTO OF THIS
PERSON HERE.

YOU ADMIRE MOST NOW

PLACE A PHOTO OF THIS
PERSON HERE.

YOU LEARNED THE MOST FROM

PLACE A PHOTO OF THIS
PERSON HERE.

HAS INSPIRED YOU THE MOST

PLACE A PHOTO OF THIS
PERSON HERE.

PLACE A PHOTO OF THIS
PERSON HERE.

HAS BEEN YOUR MOST INFLUENTIAL ROLE MODEL OR MENTOR

PLACE A PHOTO OF THIS
PERSON HERE.

PUT PHOTOS AND MEMENTOS
ON THIS PAGE.

STORIES

What is your favorite story to tell about yourself?

_____

_____

_____

_____

_____

_____

_____

What is your favorite story to tell about our family?

_____

_____

_____

_____

_____

_____

Tell me about your happiest memory.

Tell me about a difficult time in your life.

What is your earliest memory?

_____

_____

_____

_____

_____

_____

_____

Tell me about an embarrassing or funny moment.

_____

_____

_____

_____

_____

_____

_____

What was your favorite bedtime story as a child?

_____

_____

_____

_____

_____

_____

_____

What is a joke that you like to tell?

_____

_____

_____

_____

_____

_____

_____

LOOKING BACK

What have you found to be most important in life?

_____

_____

_____

_____

_____

_____

What do people tend to make a big deal about that really isn't that important after all?

_____

_____

_____

_____

_____

_____

What values do you cherish most?

....

....

....

....

....

What principles guide you?

....

....

....

....

....

What are sources of strength or support in your life?

....

....

....

....

....

LOOKING FORWARD

What do you hope the world will be like?

....

....

....

....

....

....

What experiences do you hope I will have?

....

....

....

....

....

....

What are your dreams for me?

_____
_____
_____
_____
_____
_____
_____
_____
_____

What's something you want to make sure I know?

_____
_____
_____
_____
_____
_____
_____
_____

WORDS TO LIVE BY

When you're scared . . .

When you're facing a tough decision . . .

When life throws you a curveball . . .

When you're uncertain about the future . . .

When you've lost something or someone important . . .

When you fall in love . . .

When you find your first job . . .

When you have children or grandchildren of your own . . .

_____

_____

_____

When . . .

_____

_____

_____

_____

Never . . .

_____

_____

_____

_____

Always . . .

_____

_____

_____

_____

MORE MEMORIES, PHOTOS, AND MEMENTOS

Use these pages to share more stories, record anything else that you want to tell me, or continue your entries from a previous page.

ADD MORE PHOTOS AND MEMENTOS
ON THE NEXT FEW PAGES.

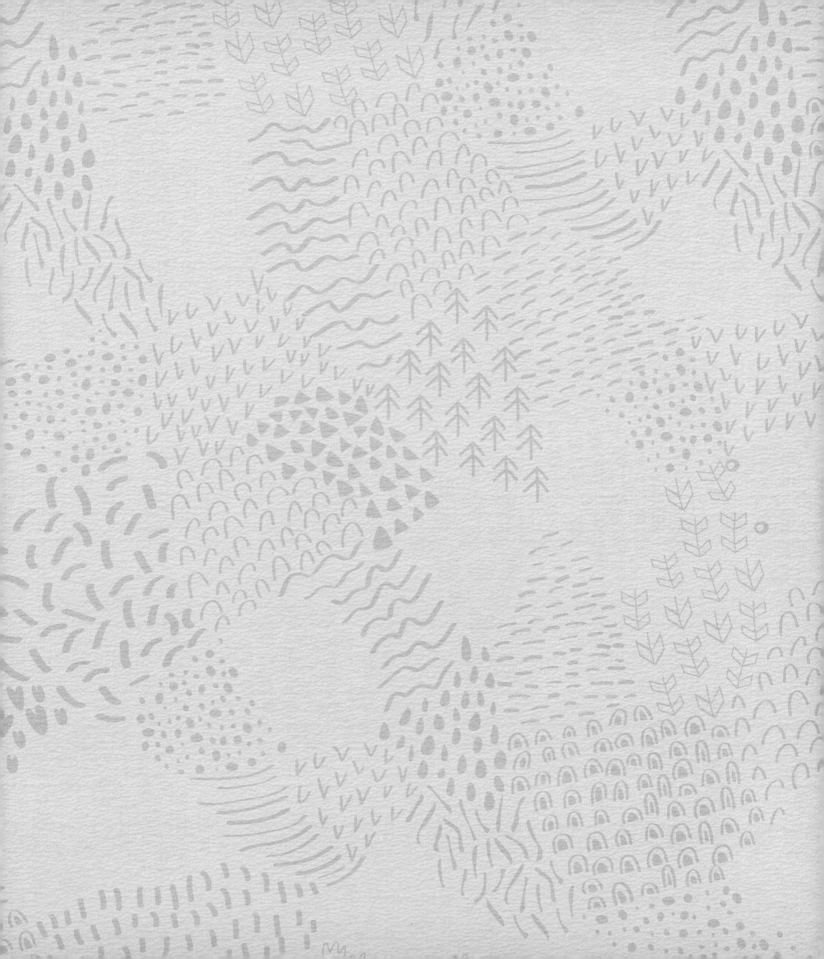

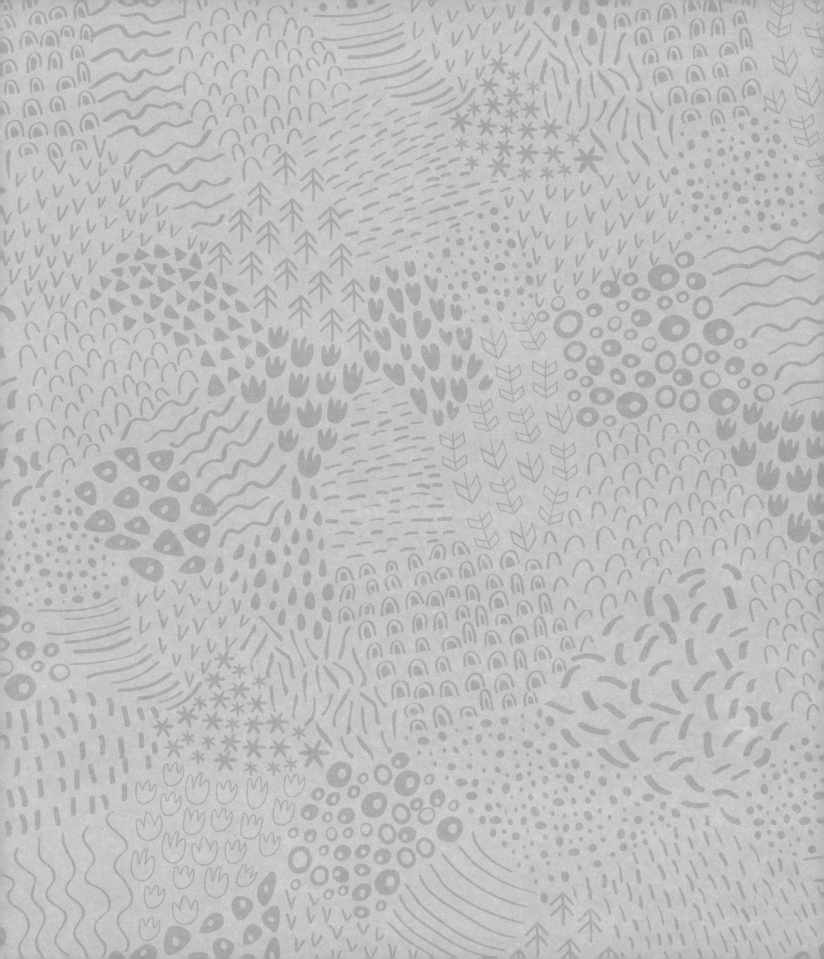